THE BEST
DOGS
EVER

SAINT BERNARDS ARE THE BEST!

Elaine Landau

LERNER PUBLICATIONS COMPANY · MINNEAPOLIS

For Jeanne Kraus

Lerner Publications Company
A division of Lerner Publishing Group, Inc.
241 First Avenue North
Minneapolis, MN 55401 U.S.A.

Website address: www.lernerbooks.com

Library of Congress Cataloging-in-Publication Data

Landau, Elaine.
    Saint Bernards are the best! / by Elaine Landau.
      p.   cm. — (The best dogs ever)
Includes index.
    ISBN 978-0-7613-6080-3 (lib. bdg. : alk. paper)
    1. Saint Bernard dog—Juvenile literature. I. Title.
SF429.S3L36 2011
636.73—dc22   2010027978

Manufactured in the United States of America
1 — CG — 12/31/10

TABLE OF CONTENTS

CHAPTER ONE

YOUR DREAM DOG

What's your
dream dog?
Is it a large, powerful
pooch? What if this dog
was also smart, friendly, and
playful? Does that sound like
the perfect pet to you? If so,
you might want to know more
about the Saint Bernard, or
Saint for short.

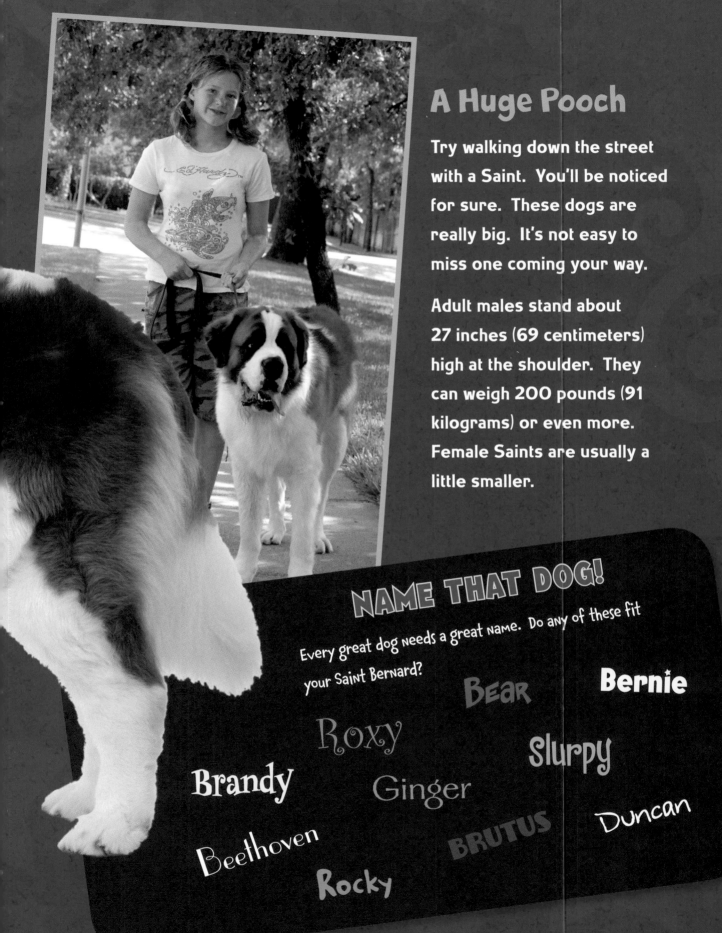

A Huge Pooch

Try walking down the street with a Saint. You'll be noticed for sure. These dogs are really big. It's not easy to miss one coming your way.

Adult males stand about 27 inches (69 centimeters) high at the shoulder. They can weigh 200 pounds (91 kilograms) or even more. Female Saints are usually a little smaller.

NAME THAT DOG!

Every great dog needs a great name. Do any of these fit your Saint Bernard?

Bear

Bernie

Roxy

Slurpy

Brandy

Ginger

Duncan

Beethoven

BRUTUS

Rocky

Saint Bernards have a look all their own. These dogs have large, wide heads with drooping cheeks. Their backs and chests are broad and muscular. Their eyes are small and dark.

Different Coats for Different Saints

A Saint Bernard's coat may be long or short. These dogs come in different colors as well. Some are mostly white with red markings. Others are mostly red with white markings. Still others are white and brindle. *Brindle* means "brown with black streaks."

The dog above is white with red markings. The dog on the left is red with white markings.

Wonderful Woofers

Saints are not just big and beautiful. They are also terrific dogs. These pooches are loving and loyal. They are kind, calm, and even tempered too.

Saints make great companions. They enjoy being with humans. Their owners think they have the best dogs ever!

BIG AND BEAUTIFUL

Don't care for skinny dogs? Then a Saint just might be perfect for you. According to *Guinness World Records*, the heaviest dog in the world was a Saint. The pooch's name was Brandy.

Brandy lived in Great Britain in the 1960s. In February 1966, Brandy weighed in at 259 pounds (117 kg). That's one huge hunk of a dog!

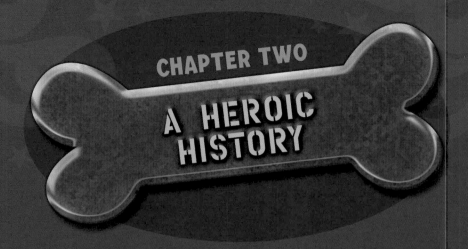

CHAPTER TWO
A HEROIC HISTORY

Saint Bernards have a proud past. They come from Switzerland. Saint Bernards were true heroes in Switzerland. As early as the 1600s, they worked as search and rescue dogs there.

This artwork from 1880 shows search and rescue Saints in Switzerland.

Search and rescue dogs help
to find people after disasters.
Saint Bernards helped to find
people who were lost in the
Swiss Alps (a mountain range)
after blizzards. With their keen
sense of smell, the dogs were
able to find people who'd been
buried under the snow. These
strong canines even dug the
victims out themselves.

In the artwork on the
right and the photo
below, Saints work to help
people after disasters.

The Saints' job wasn't easy. Often the dogs worked through thick fog and heavy snow. But they did not give up. Through the years, they rescued thousands of people.

BRAVE BARRY

The most famous Saint was a search and rescue dog named Barry. Barry lived in the Swiss Alps, where he saved more than forty people. But in 1812, he was nearly killed doing his job.

It happened while Barry was trying to dig a man out of the snow. The man didn't realize that he was being rescued. He thought Barry was a wolf and stabbed him several times.

Barry was hurt, but he survived. He was allowed to retire after that. He spent the rest of his life relaxing and being cared for. Barry died in 1814, but his heroic actions will never be forgotten.

On the Road

Saints were brought to Great Britain in the 1800s. By the 1870s, they were extremely popular in Britain. They often won prizes at dog shows. These oversized canine cuties were a hit in the United States too. Americans loved their size and sweetness. They found that these pooches were more than just good show dogs. They also made great pets.

A girl stands next to her
pet Saint Bernard in 1904.

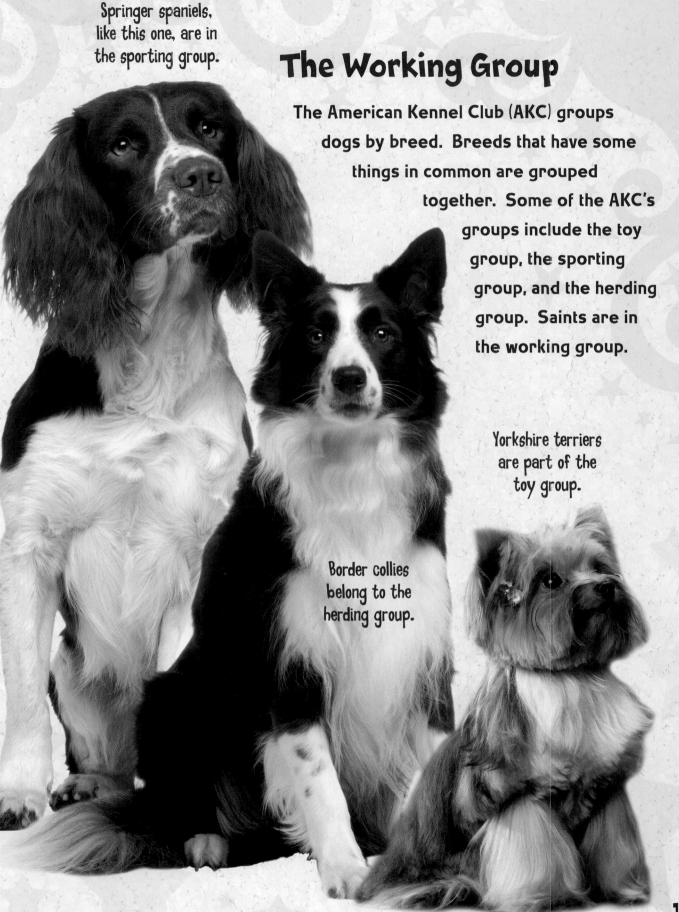

Springer spaniels, like this one, are in the sporting group.

The Working Group

The American Kennel Club (AKC) groups dogs by breed. Breeds that have some things in common are grouped together. Some of the AKC's groups include the toy group, the sporting group, and the herding group. Saints are in the working group.

Yorkshire terriers are part of the toy group.

Border collies belong to the herding group.

Dogs in the working group are large, muscular, and powerful. They also tend to be quite smart. These dogs have helped many humans through the years.

A Saint Bernard helps his owner pull a milk cart up a hill.

BEETHOVEN

A BIG HIT ON THE BIG SCREEN

Saints can be movie stars! Just check out any of the six Beethoven movies and see for yourself. In these flicks, a family tries to keep up with the adventures of their Saint Bernard named Beethoven. Saints bring smiles both on and off the screen.

CHAPTER THREE

THE RIGHT DOG FOR YOU?

So you want a Saint. Who wouldn't want such a loyal and loving dog? Having a Saint couldn't be bad. Or could it? Read on to see if a Saint is really right for you.

Is Bigger Always Better?

Giant dogs take up lots of space. You'll have less room in your house and car with a Saint. An adult Saint may weigh nearly three times as much as you.

Saints also like to be really close to their owners. Don't be surprised if your huge pooch wants to sit on your feet. These dogs also like to lean against their owners' legs. They are just being loving— but ouch!

Would you mind a large dog cuddling up close to you?

Got Time for a Needy Dog?

Saints need to be around people. They do not do well when left alone for too long. A lonely Saint can become upset. When that happens, the unhappy dog may chew on the furniture or bark for hours.

Do you have lots of after-school and weekend activities? Do the adults in your family work outside the home? Then think about getting tropical fish instead.

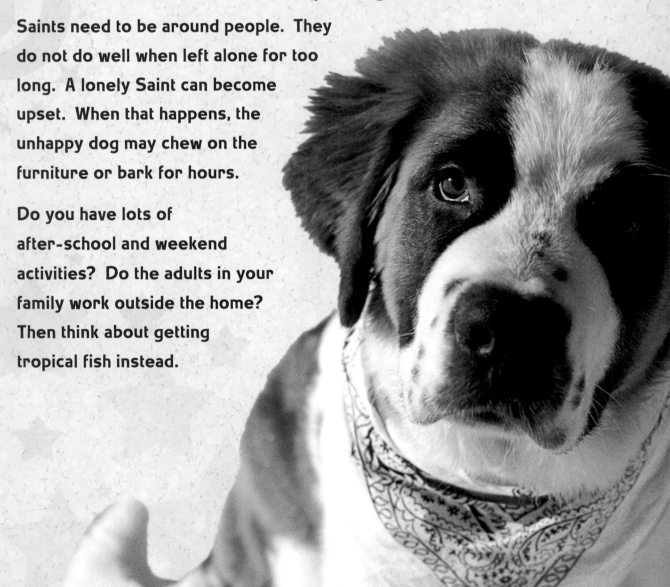

Beddy-Bye with Your Big Buddy

Will your dog sleep at the foot of your bed? If so, you'd better be a sound sleeper. Saints have been known to snore quite loudly. Your darling doggie may keep you up all night.

NOT A DOG FOR THE TROPICS

Saints do best in cooler areas. These dogs love to romp in the snow. They enjoy pulling sleds too. If you live in a very warm place, this isn't the dog for you.

Get Ready for Waterworks

Would you mind
a drippy dog?
All Saints drool
and slobber. If
you want a Saint,
you better start
collecting rags and
old towels!

The Saint Bernard
below gives its
owner a sloppy kiss.

A Pricey Pooch

Saints are purebred dogs.
Purebred puppies are quite
costly. Can you afford one?
Talk this over with your family.

RESCUE A SAINT

Can't afford a high-priced puppy? How about getting an older Saint instead? You can find these dogs at rescue centers for this breed. They often go to good homes for a small fee.

Just remember: All dogs are expensive. Even if your new pet doesn't cost very much, your family still will need to pay for its food, health care, chew toys, and more. But adopting a rescue dog can help you cut down on the purchase price.

Have you decided if a Saint's for you? If it is, a wonderful pet is coming your way. Saints are fun to be around. They also do well with little kids and other family pets. It would be hard to find a better canine companion!

CHAPTER FOUR

WELCOMING YOUR WOOFER

The big day is here! It's better than your birthday. It's more exciting than the last day of school. You're finally getting your dog.

Be Ready

You want the day to be perfect. You've got your camera ready. But you'll have to have more than that. Not sure what you'll need to welcome Fido to your family? This basic list is a great place to start.

- collar
- leash
- tags (for identification)
- dog food
- food and water bowls
- crates (one for when your pet travels by car and one for it to rest in at home)
- treats (to be used in training)
- toys

Every Dog Needs a Vet

Take your pooch to a veterinarian right away. That's a doctor who treats animals. They are called vets for short.

START TRAINING EARLY

Any large, powerful pooch must learn limits as a puppy. It must learn basic commands, such as come, sit, and stay. It also must learn not to jump up on people.

Luckily, Saints are easy to train. They want to please their owners.

The vet will check your dog's health and give it the shots it needs. Be sure to take your dog back to the vet for regular checkups. Also take your dog to the vet if it becomes ill.

A vet checks out a Saint's teeth to make sure they are healthy.

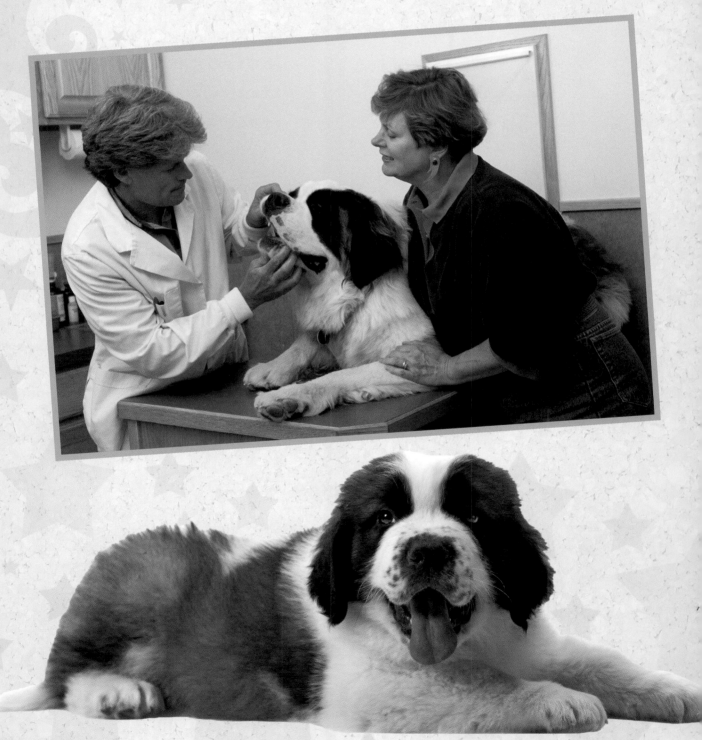

Feeding Time!

Ask your vet what to feed your dog. Dogs need different food at different stages of their lives. Keep your pet on a proper diet. Skip the table scraps. They can lead to an unhealthful weight gain.

Don't forget to fill your Saint's food and water bowls. Young puppies need to eat four meals a day.

GET ACTIVE WITH YOUR POOCH

Play ball with your Saint. Take it for long walks in the park. Run with it in the snow. You'll both have fun and get some good exercise!

Good Grooming Counts

Brush your Saint twice a week. This will remove any dead hair. It will also help prevent matting.

Take time out from your activities to keep your Saint's coat looking nice.

You and Your Special Friend

Your Saint will be a super friend. Be a good friend to your dog as well. Make sure your Saint is fed, walked, and loved every day. You just may have the best dog ever. So try to be the best dog owner ever!

GLOSSARY

American Kennel Club (AKC): an organization that groups dogs by breed. The AKC also defines the characteristics of different breeds.

breed: a particular type of dog. Dogs of the same breed have the same body shape and general features.

brindle: brown with black streaks

canine: a dog, or having to do with dogs

coat: a dog's fur

diet: the food your dog eats

matting: severe tangling. Matting causes fur to clump together in large masses.

purebred: a dog whose parents are of the same breed

rescue center: a shelter where stray and abandoned dogs are kept until they are adopted

search and rescue dog: a dog that finds people after disasters

veterinarian: a doctor who treats animals. Veterinarians are called vets for short.

working group: a group of dogs that were bred to do different types of jobs, such as guarding property, carrying messages, or pulling sleds

FOR MORE INFORMATION

Books

Brecke, Nicole, and Patricia M. Stockland. *Dogs You Can Draw*. Minneapolis: Millbrook Press, 2010. Perfect for dog lovers, this colorful book teaches readers how to draw many popular dog breeds.

Landau, Elaine. *Your Pet Dog*. Rev. ed. New York: Children's Press, 2007. This title is a good guide for young people on choosing and caring for a dog.

Markle, Sandra. *Animal Heroes: True Rescue Stories*. Minneapolis: Millbrook Press, 2009. Markle tells how dogs and other animals have helped humans in dangerous situations.

Wendorff, Anne. *Saint Bernards*. Minneapolis: Bellwether Media, 2010. Check out this book for an interesting introduction to Saint Bernards.

Websites

American Kennel Club
http://www.akc.org
Visit this website to find a complete listing of AKC-registered dog breeds, including the Saint Bernard. This site also features fun printable activities for kids.

FBI Working Dogs
http://www.fbi.gov/fun-games/kids/kids-dogs
This fun site explains all about working dogs and tells how canine crime fighters help the FBI.

LERNER *e* SOURCE™

Expand learning beyond the printed book. Download free, complementary educational resources for this book from our website, www.lernersource.com.

Index

Photo Acknowledgments

The images in this book are used with the permission of: backgrounds © iStockphoto.com/Julie Fisher and © iStockphoto.com/Tomasz Adamczyk; © iStockphoto.com/Michael Balderas, p. 1; © Ron Kimball/www.kimballstock.com, p. 4 (top); © Juniors Bildarchiv/Alamy, p. 4 (bottom); © Fiona Green, pp. 5, 17 (top), 22, 23, 25 (bottom), 28 (both); © 2007 Emmanuelle Bonzami. Image from Bigstock.com, p. 6; © Labat-Rouquette/www.kimballstock.com, p. 7 (bottom); © Alan & Sandy Carey/Photolibrary, p. 7 (top); © Bob Winsett/Photolibrary p. 8; © The Print Collector/Photolibrary, p. 9; © George Pickow/Stringer/Hulton Archive/Getty Images, p. 10 (bottom/left); Mary Evans Picture Library, pp. 10 (top/right), 11, 12, 14 (both); © Issele/Dreamstime.com, p. 13 (left); © Eric Isselée/Shutterstock Images, p. 13 (middle); © Jszg005/Dreamstime.com, p. 13 (right); © Yann Arthus-Bertrand/CORBIS, p. 15; © moodboardRF/Photolibrary, p. 16; © Juniors Bildarchiv/Alamy, p. 17; © iStockphoto.com/Michael Chen, p. 17 (bottom); © Eriklam/Dreamstime.com, p. 18 (top); © Vicky Kasala/Photodisc/Getty Images, p. 18, 20 (bottom), 29; © Justin Pumfrey/Taxi/Getty Images, p. 19; © Katrina Brown/Dreamstime.com, pp. 20 (top), 21 (top); © Myrleen Ferguson Cata/Photo Network/Alamy, p. 21 (bottom); © Tierfotoagentur/B. Schwob/Alamy, p. 24 (bottom); © Tammy Mcallister/Dreamstime.com, p. 24 (top); © April Turner/Dreamstime.com, p. 24 (second from top); © iStockphoto.com/orix3, p. 24 (third from top); © Custom Medical Stock Photo/Alamy, p. 25 (top); © Purestock/Alamy, p. 26 (top); © Katrina Brown/Alamy, p. 26 (bottom); © PatitucciPhoto/Getty Images, p. 27.

Front Cover: © Shawn And Sue Roberts/Dreamstime.com.
Back Cover: © Eric Isselée/Dreamstime.com.